Ancient Egypt

A Captivating Guide to Egyptian History, Ancient Pyramids, Temples, Egyptian Mythology, and Pharaohs such as Tutankhamun and Cleopatra

Free Bonus from Captivating History (Available for a Limited time)

Hi History Lovers!

Now you have a chance to join our exclusive history list so you can get your first history ebook for free as well as discounts and a potential to get more history books for free! Simply visit the link below to join.

Captivatinghistory.com/ebook

Also, make sure to follow us on:

Twitter: @Captivhistory

Facebook: Captivating History:@captivatinghistory

Contents

Introduction

When we think of ancient Egypt, the first things that cross our mind are mummies and pyramids, as well as the mysterious death of Tutankhamun. But that is merely a beginning. There are so many more fascinating things to discover and explore. Year after year, new excavations reveal amazing artifacts, such as clay objects that still display the fingerprints of ancient artisans. Other items help us discover the particular diseases an individual suffered from before he or she got mummified. So many small insights help us get to know ancient Egyptians—their daily lives, their drives, and motivations, emotions and weaknesses that are just like ours.

Numerous texts that have been discovered help us understand how the king, priests, and ordinary people lived and what they believed in. Those people created an incredible civilization. Their generals fought numerous battles. Their priests honored a pantheon of nearly 1,000 gods. Their kings created great architectural wonders — pyramids and a range of palaces, temples, villages, and arcane tombs.

The Ancient Egyptian Empire lasted for 3,000 years. Like many sovereign kingdoms, it emerged from the ruins that had left after the clashes of diverse forces that controlled fragmented territories, and developed into a nation that transformed North Africa and the surrounding world. Ancient Egypt gradually grew into a cultural epicenter, in which science and magic existed completely interconnected. The heights of human achievement in those golden ages are comparable to those of Ancient Greek and Roman societies at their peaks.

Those accomplishments occurred over a long period. Long before Assyrians, Persians, Greeks, and Romans subsequently invaded the country, Egyptians rose and fell entirely by themselves. There are the three major eras in the timeline of Ancient Egypt: the Old Kingdom, the Middle Kingdom, and the New Kingdom. The iconic monuments that have persisted millennia were built during the Old Kingdom. That was the time of cultural awakening and colossal construction. The Middle Kingdom was the period when a nation was united and reestablished. The New Kingdom was the time of aggressive expansion and cultural advancement.

Rather than being just an era of military triumph and expansion, the period when Egyptians shook the world was also a time of great innovation. They developed one of the first written languages (alongside Mesopotamia), invented papyrus centuries before the Chinese made paper, and originated the basic calendar structure that we still use today. Moreover, the Ancient Egyptians formulated early forms of cosmetics, including even eye makeup, and breath mints.

One of the most fascinating and sophisticated civilizations in the known history, the Ancient Egyptians are remembered by their gods, pyramids, pharaohs, mummification, hieroglyphs, agriculture and much more. This book reveals the secrets of the captivating world of Ancient Egypt, the intriguing stories of its celebrities, such as the Akhenaten, Ramses the Great, Queen Cleopatra, and the boy-king Tut. You'll learn about mighty gods and the magical link between the Sun and the people of Egypt, and explore the horrendous burial rituals that warranted a safe path to the afterlife. Find out the secrets of one of the most magnificent societies that ever existed and discover why it still manages to seize the attention of the world.

Chronology Issues

It is almost impossible to apply specific dates to eras, reigns, battles, or ceremonies. The Egyptians did not use a centralized dating system. Instead, they referred to dates in regnal years of a king (e.g. year 3 of Ramses III or year 12 of Akhenaten), which still produces confusion and discrepancies between different historical sources.

In the third century BC, the Egyptian historian and priest Manetho invented the dynastic system, which—with some modifications—we still use today. He divided the Egyptian kings into 31 dynasties, grouped them into three kingdoms and three 'intermediate' periods between them. *Important*

- Early dynastic period: Dynasty 0–2, around 3150–2686 BC
- Old Kingdom: Third to sixth dynasties, around 2686–2181 BC
- First intermediate period: Seventh to tenth dynasties, around 2181–2040 BC
- Middle Kingdom: 11th to 12th dynasties, around 2040–1782 BC
- Second intermediate period: 13th to 17th dynasties, around 1782–1570 BC
- The New Kingdom: 18th to 20th dynasties, around 1570–1070 BC
- Third intermediate period: 21st to 26th dynasties, around 1080–525 BC
- Late period: 27th to 30th dynasties, around 525–332 BC[i]

The Kingdoms and Dynasties of Ancient Egypt: A Magnificent Empire and the Dark Side

Writing and kingship were two powerful signs of progress that enabled pharaonic civilization and distinguished it from other ancient cultures. The spectacular artifacts and abundant written record about the lives, deaths, and power of Egyptian pharaohs dominate our view of its history. We know its amazing works of art and cultural achievements. However, despite numerous written and other sources, we still know so little of the daily lives of ordinary citizens. That is why the renowned contemporary Egyptologist Tobi Wilkinson points out that ancient Egypt had a darker side.[ii] There is plenty of evidence for the sinister side of pharaonic civilization. From human sacrifice in the First Dynasty to a peasants' revolt under the Ptolemies, ancient Egypt was a culture in which the relationship between the monarch and his people was based on oppression and terror, not love and admiration. King's power was absolute, and human life was cheap.

The first sovereigns in the Valley of Kings had quickly learned to use—and abuse—the remarkable power of ideology, as well as iconography, its visual counterpart. They managed to unite different groups and communities and bind them in loyalty to the pharaoh and his empire. First kings invented and utilized the tools of leadership that are still used in modern societies. Elaborate systems of symbols and wisely arranged public appearances helped isolate the ruler from the masses. Spectacular ceremonies on formal occasions served to fortify bonds of loyalty. Patriotic eagerness was regularly expressed, both orally and visually. Those means were supported by others, less benign strategies to maintain their grip on power. The strength of a king was increased by political propaganda, which reinforced an ideology of xenophobia. The population was closely monitored and dissent was brutally repressed.

The ancient Egyptians conceived the notion of the nation-state that still dominates the world. The Egyptians' concept was extraordinary, for both impact and longevity: the pharaonic state, as originally formed, lasted for three thousand years. Note that Rome barely survived one thousand year, while Western culture has yet to endure two.

Chapter 1 – Who Were Ancient Egyptians— Their Origins, History, and Geography

The Nile

The single most important entity that made the ancient Egyptian civilization possible was the Nile. The river made the life—and development—possible in an otherwise dry and desolate north-African desert. That is why Ancient Egypt is also known as the Nile valley. Because the Nile flows from south to north, the southern part of the country is counterintuitively called Upper Egypt, and the northern part is called Lower Egypt. Between July and October every year, the Nile flooded. The land on both banks was covered with water, which later receded, leaving the land covered with very fertile black silt. The Egyptians called their country the Black Land or Kemet. The Delta (the northern area where the Nile splits up into multiple canals that lead to the Mediterranean) was extraordinarily fertile. Papyrus grew there in large quantity. Agriculture flourished. However, there was always a risk of the Nile flooding excessively or insufficiently. Neither was good, as crop failure would result in famine and death.

The People

The Nile valley was a home to numerous ethnic groups of diverse origins. Before 5000 BC, the valley was inhabited by various nomadic tribes, both hunters and gatherers. Then a major climatic change caused the drying out of the area around what was to become the ancient Egypt Empire. The drought affected the populaces of large animals and further impacted the people who still had to find food and fresh water. Because of all this, the tribes came together from different directions and settled on the Nile valley, creating a whole new society. The Egyptian culture emerged from this range of diverse communities and languages.

The Development of Egyptian Society

The first settled communities led the Badarian way of life. These pastoral semi-nomads experienced numerous challenges over centuries, but things really started to accelerate when they all had to come together along the Nile valley. The abundance of resources created an interest for personal enhancement, and gradual stratification of society started to happen. People had become leaders and followers; a small ruling class had emerged and started to lead a much larger group of subjects. The rich grew richer and started funding a whole new class: specialist craftsmen. These professionals developed new technologies and products for their patrons. Only the rich had access to these prestige products, as well as other goods and materials.

Economic, cultural, and political changes were inevitable. The bunch of communities around the Nile valley had transformed into a complex society. The next step was the one towards the kingdom.

Unified Kingdom – The Legacy of King Narmer

The final drying out of the deserts around 3600 led to a sudden increase of population around the valley. Food production was intensified, urbanization was accelerated. Resources had become scarce, and the competition grew more substantial, which led to the development of first walled towns.

The people of what was to become a great kingdom were grouped in three regional groupings, with centers in the town of Tjeni (near modern Girga), Nubt (modern Nagada), and Nekhen. Each of them has its own ruler—probably a hereditary monarch. The rulers of the three groups wanted to demonstrate and enhance their authority by all means. Over time, their thirst for rare and precious objects grew. These kings wanted to own gold and precious stones, such as lapis lazuli. Because of this, both internal and external trade flourished. But this was not the only consequence. The rulers of three kingdoms saw each other as rivals, and the conflict was inevitable.

The rulers of Tjeni had a great advantage, as they already controlled two-thirds of the Egypt territory. Moreover, they had access to local harbors and established trade with Near East. After almost two centuries of antagonism, the king Narmer of Tjeni assumed the kingship of a united Egypt in around 2950. He commissioned an impressive ceremonial palette—the famous Narmer Palette—decorated with the scenes of his triumph, and devoted it in the temple at Nekhen, where it remained until its retrieval from the mud almost five millennia later.

Narmer has become the first king of the First Dynasty, the very first ruler of a united Egypt. The famous artifact from his age, the Narmer Palette, reveals a remarkable mastery of stone carving, and it shows already sophisticated art and royal iconography.

King Narmer / The Narmer Palette (Detail)

Besides revealing the artistic mastery of ancient Egyptian artisans, the Narmer Palette displays an exciting, obscure, and mysterious iconography that links Narmer's regime with a remote prehistoric past. Entwined creatures with long twisting necks, a bull crushing the walls of an enemy fortress, and other representations of forces of nature tell us much about the position of a king in early Egypt. The fact that Egyptian monuments and artifacts are made of stone is also significant: it implies permanence and immortality. Egyptian monuments were made to last forever.

Why were the iconography, monuments, and the written word so important?

The unification of Egypt was actually the creation of the world's first nation-state. The ancient Egyptians invented nationality—a common, shared identity for many different groups of people. Narmer managed to set up a governmental structure, collective values, and a very distinctive sense of Egyptian-ness.

The Egyptians invented regalia, such as crown and scepter, and they used architecture as a symbol of royal might. Despite the fact that ancient Egyptians developed a written language, the great majority of the population was illiterate. Because of that, iconography and architecture were extremely useful. On the other hand, a small class of literate people could pose a threat to the monarch. They were high officials and his closest advisors, and he needed to keep them on his side.

Hieroglyphs were extremely important too. Although they initially served an utterly mundane purpose—to facilitate record keeping—the ancient Egyptians were aware of the high ideological potential of written word. That is why they left inscriptions that contain their names, titles, and hierarchy everywhere.

The king of Two Lands

From Narmer to Cleopatra, a ruler who sought to be recognized as a true king (or queen) of Egypt had to balance and rule the opposites: Upper and Lower Egypt; the black and the red land; the realm of the living and the one of the dead. A true king of Egypt had to manage both sacred and secular aspects of life. Just as he was the head of state, he was also a god on earth.

Geography

Ancient Egypt was divided into Upper and Lower Egypt, as well as into the east and west, with the Nile as a border. The cities from the Predynastic period, such as Naqada, Hierakonpolis (Nekhen) and Abydos were all capitals at the time. However, during the Old Kingdom, one town had become the administrative capital. It was Memphis. All the royal cemeteries of the Old Kingdom, including the pyramid fields at Giza, were in close proximity. Much later, during the New Kingdom, Thebes (modern Luxor) became the new capital. To be more precise, Thebes turned into the religious capital, while Memphis remained the administrative one, ensuring the control over both Upper and Lower Egypt.

Chapter 2 – Who Held the Power: The Social Structure of Ancient Egypt

The ancient Egyptian society was highly stratified, and it could be well represented as a pyramid with the king at the top and the working class at the bottom. Right below the king were the priests, followed by a slightly bigger group of the ruling elite. The working class was at the bottom and it included a wide range of individuals, from highly skilled professionals, to utterly uneducated agricultural workers. They all had their defined place in this highly organized society.

The Pharaoh

Whether a regular heir or a usurper of the throne, the king was immensely powerful. His roles and functions, as well as responsibilities, were diverse. He was the high priest of each and every temple in the country. King was also head of the army in times of peace and war, and an international diplomat who signed peace treaties as well as trade arrangements. One of his roles was particularly interesting – the king served as an intermediary between the people and the gods. He held the title of Horus, an earthly incarnation of the highest divine existence. In short, an Egyptian king was a god himself. He was supposed to be able to talk directly with other gods, on behalf of the people of Egypt. One of his greatest responsibilities was to keep the gods happy. This was at times highly inconvenient. If the people of Egypt were afflicted with famine, war, or disease, it meant that the king was being punished.

The Priests and Elite

The position of a priest warranted a lot of power. The priests received many gifts and could become incredibly rich. They worked for the temple on the king's behalf, ensuring that the gods were satisfied, and the people were safe.

Local officials had power too. *Nomarchs*, or mayors, were in charge of their province or *nome*. They managed the economy, employment, and largely influenced the lives of people living in their territory. The nomarchs had a crucial role at times of war. Before the full-time army was introduced in the New Kingdom, the local leaders were responsible for recruiting and training healthy and strong young men from their nomes to fight for Egypt or to accompany the king on expeditions. As the military power was highly decentralized, the king had to keep good relationships with the nomarchs, he kept them on his side through presents and payments, and they became even more powerful in turn.

The second most powerful man after the king was the vizier. His responsibilities combined the ones of a state secretary and the ones of a personal assistant. The vizier compiled reports on all the important data for the whole of the country. He could do many things on the king's behalf, like distributing land and goods won at war to nomarchs or other officials, as prizes for their loyalty. The vizier was the head of justice, too. He presided over the court and dealt with the petitions, crimes and minor offenses on a daily basis.

The shift in power was common in ancient Egypt. Sometimes the vizier, a priest or other official surpassed the king in power. Ramses XI of the 20th dynasty was the high priest of Amun before he ended up on the throne. Furthermore, the priests of his time held more power than he did. The king Ay of the 18th dynasty was a vizier, and Horemheb was an army general, just like his successor, Ramses I.

The disproportion of wealth and power is evident on the tombs and pyramids that were built at the end of the Old Kingdom. The royal pyramids are smaller and less expensive than the ones of high state officials.

The Lives of Ordinary People

The remains of several villages, such as Deir el Medina, Kahun, Pi-Ramses, Avaris, and Amarna provide valuable information on how local people lived and worked. It is interesting to know that all houses in ancient people were crowded with people. The houses (or mansions) of the elite were home to the owner and his family, but also for employees, servants, and administrators. However, they consisted of many rooms and corridors, which gave the owners sufficient privacy. In small houses of the working class, on the other hand, privacy was impossible. Couples had up to 15 children, and many generations shared the same four-roomed dwellings.

The working class was large and diverse. From agricultural workers who plowed the land for the wealthy and essentially worked for survival to well-paid scribes and privileged craftsmen – there was an abundance of different occupations an Egyptian could hold.

Education

Not many Egyptian boys could choose a career in ancient times, but they prepared for one from early age. It was a norm for the oldest son in a family to follow the father's footsteps and start learning farming, sculpting, or administration as soon as he's 5 years old. Other sons had to be useful too. They were trained by professionals in different careers, and some were well educated.

The elite, as well as particularly talented boys from the working class, were taught in formal temple and palace schools. Some of these schools were highly specialized and only accepted children from families of specific occupations. There was also a local alternative for boys who were not accepted into the elite schools.

Village scribes sometimes taught local kids as well as their own children.

Girls were rarely educated. They were not accepted into formal educational institutions, as women were not permitted to hold administrative positions. Some of them were taught reading and writing, mostly because they were the daughters of scribes, but they were rare.

Five-year-olds learned reading, writing, and arithmetic. By the age of 9, all young Egyptians had to choose their career. An interesting text called the Satire of Trades[iii] describes different trades in a negative light, promoting the advantages of the profession of the scribe. Written in the form of advice of the scribe Dua-Kheti to his son, it reveals the attitude of the scribal class towards manual workers. It, however, still serves as an invaluable source of information about the careers that Egyptian boys could choose.

The Careers

There were four main categories: manual work, administration, priesthood, and military service. All careers fell into one of these categories. Not everyone could become a priest, but literally everyone could find employment in farming and building. In the New Kingdom, Egypt's best and brightest boys had two choices—to become a soldier or a scribe. The life of a soldier seemed both exciting and glamorous to many boys. The scribal profession, on the other hand, offered a cozy, peaceful life with no physical effort, as well as knowledge, influence, and wealth. A successful scribe could even become a vizier, and we have seen what that means. The entire palace and its internal operations, the police force, as well as justice (the vizier acted as a judge in behalf of the king) were under the vizier's control. Of course, not everyone could become a vizier, but even a most ordinary scribe managed to live well. Most people were illiterate, and they needed the services of a scribe.

The priesthood was more an inheritance than a calling, as it was traditionally passed down from father to son. The priest was a servant of the god. Priests did not have much contact with the population. Their main responsibility was to ensure the prayers, offerings, and incantations were performed appropriately.

In the New Kingdom, Egyptian boys could be trained to become career soldiers. Before that, if an army was needed, the nomarchs grouped likely young men from their districts and recruited them for the expedition or campaign.

While the craftsmen who constructed and decorated tombs in the Valley of the Kings were well paid and enjoyed numerous benefits, less skilled manual workers had to work full hours for nine out of ten days just to survive. Agricultural workers had no days off. Furthermore, they owned no land. The majority of the agricultural land was owned by the king or the temple and was rented to the farmers, who had an obligation to produce the specified grain quotas. Otherwise, they were beaten.

It is important to mention that it is not true that slaves worked on the construction of the pyramids. Those were employers who were given good compensations and bonuses that allowed them to accumulate wealth, as well as health care. There are written proofs that the highly skilled construction workers and artists who were settled in Deir el Medina and were in charge of major project in the Valley of the Kings could take as many days off as they wanted, even for a reason such as hangover—which was, surprisingly or not, one of the most common excuses.

While farmers and agricultural workers were the most impoverished members in ancient Egyptian society, their job was not the worst. The worst occupation, according to the *Satire of the Trades*, was the one of a laundryman. In a highly differentiated society of specialized professionals, such as the ancient Egypt, there was a need for professionals who would take care of people's loincloths. The laundrymen collected laundry from houses and washed it in the Nile using a simple soap made of natron and lime. Washing other men's loincloths was not only disgusting; it was also physically hard and dangerous. The clothes had to be crushed against stones in order for the stains to be removed. To make it even harder, the Nile was home to the number of crocodiles, parasitic worms, and potentially deadly biting insects.

Women

Egyptian women enjoyed a lot of freedom compared to most women in other ancient societies. They could walk around without a male companion, and had the same legal rights as men from their class. Even though they spent most of the time at home, they could earn money by selling goods they produced, such as bread, beer, linen, baskets, or vegetables. Some of them were employed in private households and held the positions that are similar to the modern role of housekeeper. Others worked as midwives—which was a lucrative and highly necessary occupation, considering the number of children in each family (usually between five and fifteen)—or wet nurses. Some of the Egyptian women were involved in the priesthood, holding various roles in the cults of goddesses such as Isis, Neith, or Hathor. Among other rights, Egyptian women could own, inherit, and bequeath property. However, royal women did not enjoy these freedoms. They were confined in the harem and were often used as political pawns. Too often, they were forced to marry a brother, the father (or an elderly vizier hungry for power, as we shall see in one of the subsequent chapters) and to engage in relationships that were far from natural, just to ensure that the throne remains within the family.

Ancient Egyptians married at very young age, and everyone was expected to have children. Weddings were informal, and so were divorces. Contrary to a popular misconception, Egyptians did not normally engage in incestuous relationships. Marriages between siblings did occasionally occur in royal families, entirely because of political reasons.

Elderly care was the responsibility of their children, especially daughters. Male children had to take care of the parents of their wives. However, some people, like the elite workers in Deir el Medina and the military, received a state pension. The average age of death was 35, due to early deaths caused by diseases or injuries, but it wasn't unusual to reach very old age, even for our terms.

Chapter 3 – On Kings and their Military Power: A Chronological Overview of Kingdoms, Dynasties, Pharaohs, and their Achievements from the Pre-dynastic Period to the New Kingdom

Egyptians kept records of their kings and their accomplishments. These records are available in the form of *king lists*, which give us testimonies about pharaohs' names and titles, reign lengths, and major events. However, these lists are selective and do not contain all pharaohs. The dates are questionable too because ancient Egyptians did not have a unique calendar.

The Pre-dynastic Period

During the pre-dynastic period (from around 5000 BC to around 3000 BC[iv]) two separate cultures existed: Upper and Lower Egypt. From the archaeological point of view, it is interesting that most Egyptian settlements were located in Lower Egypt (which was, contrary to today's common logic, on the North), while the cemeteries were positioned in Upper (southern) Egypt. The cultures of the Two Lands were a foundation to later Egyptian civilization.

King Narmer (dynasty 0) established the Egyptian civilization that we know today. He unified numerous locally governed regions using his military might. His ceremonial palette depicts the earliest battle scene ever documented in ancient Egypt. Its imagery—particularly the image of the king wearing the crown of both Upper and Lower Egypt—implies that Egypt should never be divided again. All pharaohs had to sustain this model and govern a united Egypt. The early dynastic period had started with the first dynasty and finished with the end of the second dynasty. Gradually, the state was entirely formed, and the pharaohs had started to build huge underground tombs, full of expensive goods.

The Old Kingdom – The Age of Pyramids

Even though the beginnings and early development of the Egyptian society can be tracked to the country's prehistoric past, thousands of years before the pyramids, the iconic monuments on the Giza plateau mark the first great cultural zenith of pharaonic culture. The ideology of divine kingship is what defines this period. The spreading of a belief in an emperor with divine authority was the most important triumph of Egypt's early kings. In the Egyptian consciousness, this belief became the only acceptable form of government—and it remained so for the next three thousand years. That is why this type of monarchy remained the longest-lasting political and religious system the world has ever seen. Art, writing, ceremony, and architecture of ancient Egypt all expressed the belief in this system and provided both the inspiration and the justification for colossal royal tombs.

The Old Kingdom had begun with the third dynasty (around 2686 BC), and ended with the sixth (around 2333 BC). That was the time when the great pyramids were built. The first pyramid was the one of King Djoser of the third dynasty. He built the Step Pyramid in Saqqara. The Great Pyramid of King Khufu at Giza represents the culmination of the evolution of pyramids. In the fifth dynasty, the Pyramid Texts became as important as the pyramids, and the sixth dynasty saw a decline. Floods, famine, and nobility growing richer than the kings (the tombs of the nobles are far more expensive than the ones of royals in the sixth dynasty)—all these factors marked the end of the Old Kingdom.

The First Intermediate Period

The end of the Old Kingdom was followed by a time of political unrest, called the first intermediate period. The poor rose up against the elite and the rulers. It was a time of anarchy in which people feared for their lives. According to the *Admonitions of Ipuwer*, people were afraid of their own family members. "A man regards his son as his enemy. [...] The virtuous man goes in mourning because of what has happened in the land."[v]

Egypt became divided again. The eighth dynasty's administration was located in the Memphite region, and its rule was limited to the local area. The rest of Egypt was under the control of various insignificant leaders. When the eighth dynasty collapsed, the ninth dynasty started its rule from Herakleopolis. At one point, this dynasty retrieved the power over the whole of Egypt, but it divided again during the tenth and eleventh dynasty, when the capital moved to Thebes.

The Middle Kingdom – The Age of Fortresses and Military Expeditions

Mentuhotep I, the fourth pharaoh of the 11th dynasty, managed to reunite and take control of all of Egypt around 2100 BC. This was the beginning of the period called the Middle Kingdom. The king was still dependent on local governors. He needed their help in order to raise an army. The pharaoh Senwosret III of the 12th dynasty finally gained enough power to raise an army himself.

Just like the Old Kingdom is known for magnificent pyramids, the Middle Kingdom had its fortresses. This was a period of military expansion and increase of the Egypt's territory. Every time Egyptians expanded to a new area, they built a large, impressive fortress to let the enemy know that the Egyptians were here to stay.

In the 12th dynasty, the pharaoh Amenemhat I made a row of fortresses in the northeastern Delta to defend new borders. Also, a row of 17 fortresses was constructed in Nubia, well past the borders, to prevent the entrance of Nubians and to control the gold mines trade and other activities in the region. All fortresses shared common architectural elements, such as bastions (enabled soldiers to fire on the enemy), walls made of mud brick, with walkway at the top (enabled the soldiers to patrol the border), white ditches around the walls, and walled stairways to the Nile (enabled supplying and naval attacks). Some fortresses had walled towns and temples in close proximity.

The Second Intermediate Period

The Middle Kingdom ended and the second intermediate period began around 1800 BC, in a similar way like the first: floods, famine, and anarchy. At the same time, a number of immigrants from the area of Syria and Palestine (the Egyptians referred to them as Asiatics) came and were welcomed by the government, which sought to make use of their boat-making skills. Then the *Hyksos period* started. The rule over Egypt was divided again. The 15th dynasty—the Hyksos, empowered by the Asiatic community—ruled from Avaris in the north, while the 17th dynasty held the south from Thebes. The 17th dynasty pharaohs were Egyptians, but most likely they were just vassal rulers and didn't cause any trouble to the Hyksos.

Contrary the widespread myth that the Hyksos invaded Egypt from Palestine on their chariots, such event never took place. The Hyksos rulers belonged to the local Siro-Palestinian community that had been living in the Nile Delta for more than a century before the Hyksos period began.

Even though the Hyksos managed to gain control over both Upper and Lower Egypt by approximately 1600 BC, they got expelled eventually. In the time of the Hyksos king Apophis, the 17th dynasty king Seqenenre Tao fought against them. The king from Thebes died in battle, but his son Kamose continued to fight and, after him, his brother Ahmose managed to force the enemies out of Egypt.

The New Kingdom

The New Kingdom began with Ahmose's return to Egypt, around 1550 BC. He was the first king of the 18th dynasty, and he introduced numerous changes in government and administration. Most important of all, he established a full-time permanent army.

Everybody could join the army. The training started at the age of 5, and professional service started at the age of 20. Even though just like in other occupations, military roles were passed on from father to son, others could become soldiers and increase their ranks over time. The army was split into divisions of five thousand men. Each of them was named after a god. All generals of the divisions were royal sons. If there were not enough grown-up princes available, the title of general was given to a boy-prince. Divisions were highly specialized. There were archers, spearmen, charioteers, and foreign mercenaries—to name a few. The army was additionally divided into hosts, companies, platoons, and squads. Soldiers were accompanied by camp followers, responsible for cleaning, cooking, and fetching water; trumpeters and drummers who signaled the tactic durring battles; standard bearers; and scribes who recorded the number of the enemy dead, by counting amputated body parts after a battle, as well as the number of prisoners. However, battle records are not quite reliable historical source. They were created for the purpose of propaganda. According to them, Egyptians never got hurt or killed in a battle, because they were unbeatable and scary for the enemies, who would often just run away with terror. Archeological evidence, on the other hand, shows that the reality was different. A number of mummies show the signs of battle wounds.

The introduction of permanent army changed Egypt forever, enabling the beginning of a new era. The New Kingdom grew into a true empire ruled by famous pharaohs Tutankhamun, Akhenaten, and Ramses II. Here begins one of the most interesting periods in ancient Egyptian civilization, the one that certainly deserves our close attention.

Chapter 4: The Magnificent Pharaohs of the New Kingdom and Their Empire

The New Kingdom started with successful military action and the expulsion of the Hyksos. It lasted from around 1570 to approximately 1070 BC and included the rulers from the 18th and 19th dynasties—the most powerful monarchs of the ancient world.

Not only that the 18th dynasty rulers had established a permanent army. They changed the Egypt's international policy forever. The pharaohs of the New Kingdom had set a new standard. Extending the borders had become essential and each pharaoh sought to claim larger territory than his father. As a result, a vast area of the Near East was brought under Egyptians' control. The new territories still had their own kings, but all of them were vassals loyal to Egypt.

Thutmosis III

Thutmosis III was the first Egyptian pharaoh who was fully devoted to empire building. He spent most of his life fighting and increasing the territory of Egypt. Because of this, modern Egyptologists often refer to him as the Egyptian Napoleon. His military successes are recorded in the Hall of Annals at Karnak temple.

The first Egyptian emperor was the son of Thutmosis II and his secondary wife Isis. He was still a child when his father died, leaving him the throne. Young monarch married his father first wife, Hatshepsut, who ruled the country until the king grew up. Meanwhile, he was training in the army. After 22 years of their rule,

Hatshepsut died, and Thutmosis III, now a fully grown adult and skilled military leader, took over the throne and ruled for over 20 years.

Thutmosis III (1504-1450 BC), basalt statue in Luxor Museum

The Historical Armageddon

Most people do not know that the biblical term Armageddon (literally: "mount of Megiddo," located in modern-day Israel) refers to a particular battle that took place there. There is a possibility that this actual battle was the one between Thutmosis III's forces and the king of Kadesh in Syria—and not just him. Around 1476, during the first year of Thutmosis III's solo rule, after his wife's death, the king of Kadesh gathered a number of Palestinian cities. They joined forces to attack the borders of Egypt from the town of Megiddo, which was fortified and strategically desirable. The Egyptians took the direct route to Megiddo, even though that meant they would be in a vulnerable position. The Syrian army was assembled of more than 330 kings and their forces, greatly outnumbering the Egyptian army. In spite of that, Thutmosis III appeared fearless and influenced his men to be so, too. They marched in full battle regalia to enhance their morale and induce panic in the enemy lines, and—it worked. They were powerful, and the army at Megiddo ran away rapidly, leaving all their equipment behind. However, they couldn't enter the fortress, as the gatekeepers at Megiddo refused to open the doors. Those inside the walls feared that the Egyptians would follow the Syrians in. The Egyptians, on the other hand, missed the opportunity to take over the fortification quickly, as they were too busy rummaging the weapons, chariots, and other goods the enemy left behind. At the end, it took Thutmosis and his men seven months to conquer Megiddo. The next step was to take the city of Kadesh, which was positioned on an important trade route and gave access to northern territories. At the end, as the result of these actions, both the pharaoh and his soldiers had become richer and more powerful.

Akhenaten

An equally famous 18th-dynasty king, albeit for wholly different reason, was Akhenaten. He is remembered as a heretic king, the one who changed the Egyptian religion from the worship of countless gods to the worship of a single god. This change was influenced by monotheism, but in Akhenaten's system, there were actually two gods. The pharaoh and his family had an exclusive right to worship the new god – the Aten or sun – and literally everyone else had to worship Akhenaten. While the Aten was the supreme god, Akhenaten elevated himself to the position of fully fledged deity.

Akhenaten (1350-1333 BC)[vi]

His name meant "Spirit of the Aten," but that was not the name he was given at birth. He was the youngest son of Amenhotep III, and initially, his name was Amenhotep, too. His family did not quite fit the contemporary stereotype. Not only that his mother, Tiye, was not of royal birth; she was also a domineering woman. The contemporary art depicted her alongside her husband, as his equal. In earlier Egyptian history, however, the queens were always inferior. The Akhenaten's older brother, Thutmosis, passed away before he could become a king. He had three sisters, and two of them were married to his father.

Nefertiti

No one knows exactly who she was, where she came from, or who her parents were, but she married Akhenaten and gave birth to six princesses. The girls were usually depicted with the ruling couple, which was also unusual in their tradition. Nefertiti was related to the former queen Tiye, although the link is not quite clear. All we know is that the wife of Tiye's brother Ay was the 'wet-nurse of Nefertiti.' She could have been her mother, but there's still no evidence for such hypothesis.

Nefertiti was not the only member of Akhenaten's family whose origin was covered with mystery. There is a strong possibility that Tutankhamun was his son, as Tut was the son of Kiya, Akhenaten secondary wife. Furthermore, Akhenaten's successor on the throne was the enigmatic king Smenkhkare – and no one knows who he was. He might be another Akhenaten's son, or a son of Amenhotep III, or even Nefertiti in disguise. Whoever he was, he remained on the throne for a rather short period of time.

Akhenaten managed to change the religious system of Ancient Egypt completely. It took him around nine years to complete the revolution. We know all about it because this period is most thoroughly covered, compared to other periods in ancient Egyptian history. The Aten is the critical element in the reign of Akhenaten. The Aten was not some new, unheard-of god. He has always been present as an element of the broader solar cycle, as an epitome of the light that radiates from the sun disc. This light was usually depicted by hands emanating from the sun disc. Each hand was ending in small hands that form a sign of eternal life (ankh) to the royal family. The picture implies that the sun gives life. So Akhenaten essentially just raised this element of the sun deity and promoted it into the only sun god. The religious revolution had a practical purpose. Amenhotep III started to favor the Aten over other gods because he wanted to reduce the influence of the Priesthood of Amun at Karnak. This priesthood had almost as much power as the royal family. Akhenaten went a step further and replaced all gods with the Aten. Nine years into his reign, he closed all existing temples and redirected all income to the new temples of the Aten. Three years later, Akhenaten decided to expel all the traces of the cult of Amun. The names of Amun were deleted everywhere, even in the name of Amenhotep. This was a bit too much and, most probably, a number of people were deeply upset.

Akhenaten ruled from the new city at Amarna in central Egypt. Most likely, he was a co-ruler with his father Amenhotep III, who was still situated at Thebes. Even though this was a divided rule, it was seen as acceptable.

We do not know how exactly Akhenaten died but some unfortunate and sometimes truly bizarre events preceded his death. Amenhotep III died in year 12 of Akhenaten's reign. In the next year, all signs of Nefertiti disappeared. She either died or, as some Egyptologists believe, changed her name and become a co-ruler. The year after, Akhenaten's mother, as well as one of his sisters, died. Three years later, Akhenaten died and, soon after him, the mysterious heir Smenkhkare, who ruled as a co-ruler with Akhenaten for three years and alone for a couple of months.

All these deaths were due to "the Asiatic illness," which was, in fact, a plague epidemic. The disease defeated Amarna, which was seen by the populace as punishment for the religious revolution and abandonment of the traditional gods.

Tutankhamun

When both Akhenaten and Smenkhkare died, it wasn't easy to find an heir to the throne. The only suitable one was Tutankhamun, who was only seven years old at the time. Experts are not sure who his parents were, although his father was either Akhenaten (with Kiya or Tadukhipa) or Amenhotep III (with Tiye or Sitamun). He was born in Amarna, as Tutankhaten, but his name had to be changed when he became king.

The first thing that comes to mind when we hear of the name Tutankhamun is the treasure found in his tomb. However, these artifacts may not have featured whatsoever in Tut's life. Most of them are actually created specifically for the tomb.

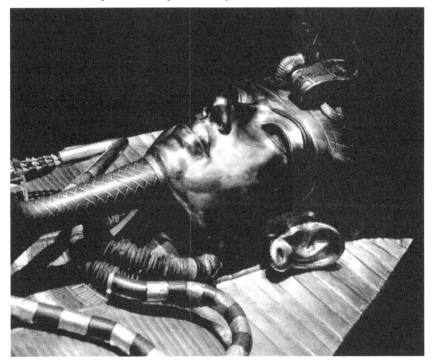

Tutankhamun's innermost coffin

Tutankhamun's wife was Ankhesenamun (born as Ankhesenepaten). The couple ruled for ten years and had no surviving children. Two female babies were found in Tutankhamun's tomb. Unfortunately, the world's most famous pharaoh did not have an heir. Many believe that, since Tutankhamun was very young, he might have been under great influence of the general and deputy king Horemheb and the vizier, Ay.

Tutankhamun abandoned Amarna and returned to traditional capitals of Egypt, Memphis, and Thebes. The Restoration Stela at Karnak temple says that he also restored the Egyptian religion and abandoned all the changes that Akhenaten had initiated.

Mysterious Death and an Unwanted Marriage

Even though a recent CT scan showed that Tutankhamun had not died from a blow to the head (the bone fractures that made everyone think the boy-king was murdered occurred long after his death), his death is still covered by a veil of mystery. Furthermore, Tut's death was followed by many intriguing events. His vizier, Ay (mentioned earlier in this chapter as the brother of Akhenaten's mother Tiye, and also peculiarly related to Nefertiti) took over the throne and was about to marry Tutankhamun's widow. Ankhesenamun was petrified with the idea, because, firstly, she despised his origin and referred to him as a servant and, secondly, because he was very old while she was in her early twenties. Perhaps there was a third reason too, maybe he had something to do with Tutankhamun's death, but we don't have any proofs at this point. The young widow-queen wrote a letter to the Hittite king Suppiluliumas, asking him to send one of his sons to Egypt. She hoped she would marry a young prince instead of the elderly servant. It took a while before the Hittite king realized she was honest in her request and sent one of his sons to Egypt. Unfortunately, the prince was killed on the way, and Ay certainly had something to do about it, as he married the unfortunate queen shortly after.

Ay was around 60 when he took the throne and ruled for only four years. The next on the throne was Horemheb, Tutankhamun's deputy king, and an army general. He ruled for 30 years and named one of his generals, Piramesis, as his successor at the throne. Ramses I (the name Piramesis took on taking the throne) was the first pharaoh of the 19th dynasty, but he only ruled for two years, leaving the throne to his son, Sety I.

The Recovery of Imperial Might: Sety I and Ramses II

A number of political problems started to emerge during the reigns of Sety I (1291-1278 BC) and his successors. The pharaohs of the previous dynasty, Akhenaten and Smenkhkare, neglected the boundaries of the decaying Egyptian empire, which needed to be re-established. As soon as he took the throne, Sety I heard that local tribal leaders were plotting rebellion, and so he entered a campaign across Syria. Sety I took the city of Kadesh, but the Hittites suppressed the Egyptians shortly after. However, the pharaoh and his army continued to take over fortified Syrian towns, either in battles, such as the one at Karnak, or through an act of surrender.

Sety's son Ramses II (also known as Ozymandias) thought it would be a great idea to claim divine birth. His parents, albeit on the throne, had a non-royal origin, and Ramses apparently saw that as a problem. Different images found at his mortuary temple at Luxor depict different gods, such as Amun or the ram-headed god Khnum, as his father. Anyway, Sety I had named his son as co-regent and they ruled together for a couple of years. Ramses was married to Nefertari, Isetnofret, and many others. He had a harem of 300 women, a present from his father. He also had numerous children. Some records show that he had 150 sons and 70 daughters, but these numbers are exaggerated. He seemed to have up to 46 sons and approximately 55 daughters. He had at least ten children with Nefertari and six of them were boys, but unfortunately, they all died before Ramses did. With Isetnofret, he had six children, and one of them had followed Ramses II on the throne. He was Ramses's 13th son, born as Merenptah.

Statue of Ramses II (1279-1212 BC), Luxor

Ramses II had earned his glory by leading a spectacular battle against the Hittites during the fifth year of his reign. This battle took place at Kadesh. Sety had triumphed at Kadesh before, but soon after that, the Hittites managed to get close to the Egyptian borders. Egypt needed to stop them by attacking them. The Hittite king had expected the assault, made a pact with many neighboring provinces, and gathered a huge army. Both sides utilized the same weapons, but the Hittite army was larger. The styles of the attack were different too. Ramses II led the division named after the god Amun. Other divisions were called Ra, Ptah, and Seth. While approaching Kadesh, the divisions split, and at one point the Amun division alone faced the Hittite forces. Most of Ramses's men died, and it was a miracle that he survived. The documents from this period say that the pharaoh fought the entire Hittite army on his own. Eventually, other divisions managed to join him and drive the enemy back. The Hittites escaped into the walled city of Kadesh, and the Egyptians claimed victory. Sixteen years later, the Egyptians and the Hittites signed a peace treaty and ended all hostilities.

Tablet of the treaty between Hattushili III of Hatti and Ramesses II of Egypt, version found in Boghazköi/ Hattusha[vii]

The Last Mighty Pharaohs: Merenptah and Ramses III

Merenptah (1212-1202 BC) was Ramses II's 13th son. His reign was marked by continuous problems with the Libyans, who joined forces with a number of other tribes. The Sea People—25000 men with their families and belongings—were traveling to Egypt and attempting to invade it. In a couple of occasions, they managed to penetrate the Egyptian fortresses and devastate the guard. Merenptah led his archers, defeated the Libyans, and took many prisoners. All that Egyptians wanted was to live peacefully without fear, and the pharaoh enabled them to do so, albeit for a short period.

The invasions continued during the reign of Merenptah's son, Ramses III (1182–1151 BC). The Sea People had grown very strong; they managed to win an important battle against the Hittites, which enabled them to control trade in the near east on both land and sea. Ramses III confronted the Sea People on both land and sea and triumphed both times. His battle on the sea is one of the earliest naval battles ever documented in history. The Egyptian fleet of ships followed the enemy's fleet into the so-called 'river-mouths of the Delta,' and trapped the Sea People between the Egyptian boats and the shore. The Egyptian archers were waiting at the shore, ready to shower them with arrows. The Sea People were devastated. But the Libyans stroke again, in year 11 of Ramses III's reign.

Ramses III was the last pharaoh to reign in true traditional style. The periods that followed were tormented by divided land, assaults, and economic breakdown. The mighty kingdom that Thutmosis III built and Sety I and Ramses II preserved was gradually declining, together with the Egyptian civilization.

Chapter 5 – The Decay and End of the Egyptian Civilization

The traditional Egyptian culture started to sink at the end of the New Kingdom. With the 20th dynasty (1185-1070 BC), this powerful and economically strong country began to fall. The throne was divided and two or more kings ruled from separate cities. It was clearly a bad sign, as a united Egypt under one pharaoh was a vital part of ancient Egyptian tradition.

Third Intermediate Period

The fall of Egypt was a gradual process that lasted for over 1000 years. The country that Ramses II and Ramses III left as a legacy was still mighty, but it slowly declined until the age of Cleopatra. The Third Intermediate period lasted from 1080 BC to 525 BC. During that time, many rulers were reigning from different regions of Egypt, even at the same time. The period that followed was Late Period. Foreign invasion and frequent changes of dynasties characterized this epoch. Finally, the Greco-Roman Period (332-30 BC), which started off with the invasion of Alexander the Great, caused some major cultural changes.

The decline didn't happen overnight, but it was clearly evident during the reign of Ramses XI (1098-1070 BC). Various economic problems were slowly reducing the power of the pharaoh. The priests of Amun, on the other hand, were multiplying their power and wealth. Eventually, they became equally powerful as the pharaoh—the only difference was that the king still had the control over the army—and that was almost entirely his own fault. Ramses XI sponsored this escalation in power through countless gifts, aids, and construction works at the temple of Karnak in Luxor.

When the conflict between the Viceroy of Nubia, Panehsy, and the high priest of Amun, Amenhotep, Ramses took the latter's side. Furthermore, the religious pharaoh helped Amenhotep's successor at the position of the high priest of Amun, Herihor, to push him out from the throne. Ramses gave him the military titles that belonged to Panehsy. Now Herihor held both religious and military titles and became unstoppable in his ambition. He occupied the role of the pharaoh while the legitimate pharaoh was still alive. Herihor happened to have died before Ramses, but his successor, Piankhy, continued to rule the same way. Piankhy became a king after Ramses died, but remained so only for a couple of months. His influence was limited to the area around Thebes, in the south.

At the same time, at the north of the country, a man of unknown origin called Smendes (1069–1043 BC) married Ramses XI's daughter and claimed the throne of Egypt. He built his own capital at Tanis, on the ruins of Pi-Ramses. The next king on this throne was Psusennes I (1039-991 BC). The most interesting thing about him was that he let his daughter marry Menkhepere, the high priest of Amun. This marriage implies that the relationships between the northern and the southern rulers were good. They remained so for the next 350 years, warranting peace and even prosperity.

Egypt was united once again during the rule of Sheshonq, who was, in fact, a Libyan chieftain. He had understood well that this unification was crucial in order for him to become a legitimate pharaoh. Moreover, he married an Egyptian princess—a daughter of Psusennes II, the last pharaoh in the 21st dynasty—and made sure his son held the title of high priest of Amun. However, the end of his 22nd dynasty was full of hostility and divisions, and even a civil war that lasted for more than ten years. During the next period, too many pharaohs (dynasties 22, 23, and 24) emerged at the same time, each ruling his own small area.

Around 727 BC, a serious threat emerged and forced the kings to work together. Nubia had become too powerful and presented a danger. The northern kings of Tanis (the 22nd dynasty), Leontopolis (the 23rd dynasty), and Sais (the 24th dynasty) united so that they could deal with the Nubian rulers (25th dynasty). The former tried to prevent the latter's control from escalating. The Nubian pharaoh at the time was Piankhy, who was, at the same time, the high priest of Amun. He and his son Shabaka managed to increase the power and gain the control over almost all of Egypt.

The next threat came from the Assyrian empire. The Assyrian king Esarhaddon entered Egypt in 671 BC, during the reign of Nubian pharaoh Taharqua. Esarhaddon's son Ashurbanipal managed to gain full control over Egypt, settle in Thebes, and become the king of Upper and Lower Egypt.

Late Period

In the next couple of decades, Egypt had vassal rulers, loyal to the Assyrian kings. New capital was Sais, and the ruling dynasty was the 26th one, also known as the Saite dynasty. However, one of the Saite rulers, Psamtik I (664-610 BC) decided he would not be a vassal king anymore. He already brought many changes, trying to reinstate past traditions. He resumed various elements of religion, ritual, and art, to show continuity with the culture of the Old and Middle Kingdoms. The next step in order to become a truly traditional pharaoh of Egypt is to set the country free from foreign influence. The Assyrians, on the other hand, had their own internal problems to deal with, and Psamtik I managed to gain control of Egypt in his own right.

Egypt was on the good track again. The next on the throne, Nekau II, further improved the status of Egypt, controlled Syria-Palestine, employed a number of Ionian Greeks and, with their help, established Egypt's first official naval service. The trade increased too, and Nekau II constructed a canal to the Red Sea. The trade relations intensified further, Egypt grew richer and a number of foreign immigrants came. They eventually started to cause problems and civil wars between different foreign groups during the reign of Ahmose II (a.k.a. Amasis; 570-526 BC).

Meanwhile, the Assyrian empire was crashed. The Persians took over Nineveh in 612 BC, continued to grow their power and territory, and eventually, in 525 BC invaded Egypt, and took the pharaoh, Psamtik III, with them as a prisoner of war. Thus started the Persian 27th dynasty, and endured for over 100 years (525-414 BC). The Persian king who originally won Egypt, Cambyses (525-522 BC), returned to Persia, leaving a local governor to rule on his behalf, but his successor Darius I (521-486 BC) got very much involved with Egypt's internal affairs. He built and repaired a number of objects, including temples and the canal to the Red Sea that the Saite king Nakau started. However, the Egyptians revolted. The next Persian king, Xerxes, finally crushed the revolt, but then the Greeks came. Egyptians, with the help of Greek mercenaries, managed to assassin Xerxes. They spent the following period trying to get rid of the Persians, while their culture and power declined further around 400. The next dynasties (the 28th, 29th, and 30th) were rather insignificant. The only ruler worth mentioning is the pharaoh Nectanebo II, the last ruler of the 30 dynasty, who fought against the Persian king Artaxerxes III and lost. He died in 343 BC as the last Egyptian ruler on the throne. All subsequent rulers were foreign. Some historians consider the Persian rulers of Egypt as the 31st dynasty (343-332 BC). This dynasty, however, lasted for a rather short period and ended in 332 BC when Darius III opened the borders to let Alexander the Great in.

Alexander the Great and the Ptolemies

Alexander's goal at the time was to defeat the Persians. However, once he entered Egypt, he was genuinely interested in becoming a pharaoh. He traveled to Siwa, where the oracle of Amun was placed, in order to legitimize his place on the throne by proving that he was the divine son, predestined to be a king of Egypt. He stayed in Egypt for a while, renovating temples, building the new capital city, Alexandria, introducing a monetary system, and so on, but eventually he moved on and continued to conquer nations throughout the region. Alexandria was a large (with a population of more than half a million), cosmopolitan city, and a home to numerous Greek and Jewish immigrants, among others. The city was completed under Ptolemy II (285-246 BC).

Alexander the Great died in 323 BC. His son Alexander IV took the throne much later, because he was born after the father's death. Meanwhile, Alexander's generals effectively ruled. Ptolemy was the governor of Egypt and, later, established a dynasty of Ptolemies. All kings were called Ptolemy, so there were 15 Ptolemies. As for the queens, there were seven Cleopatras and four Berenices on the throne (and there were certainly much more Cleopatras and Berenices in the royal family). The Ptolemaic dynasty supported the Egyptian tradition but also brought many Hellenistic elements to it. These rulers were obsessed with taking the throne and staying on it, marrying their siblings and having children with them, in order to keep the family on the throne forever. This, however, did not mean that the relations inside the family were good. The family had a huge record of plots and murders.

- Phillip Arrhidaeus (the predecessor of the first Ptolemy) was murdered by one of his bodyguards.
- Berenice II was poisoned by her son Ptolemy IV.
- Arsinoe, Ptolemy IV's wife, was killed by the brother of Agathoclea, the Ptolemy's secondary wife

- Ptolemy VII was murdered by his uncle and stepfather Ptolemy VIII

- Memphites was killed by his father, Ptolemy VIII, who subsequently sent his corpse to his wife and sister, Cleopatra II, as a birthday present.

- Cleopatra III was probably killed by her younger son, Ptolemy X (it is interesting that, prior to her death, her older son, Ptolemy IX, was indicted of conspiracy against her).

- Berenice, the daughter of Ptolemy IX, was assassinated a month after marrying Ptolemy XI, as he wasn't willing to share the throne with her.

- After 19 days, the public, appalled by the murder of the much-loved queen Berenice, lynched Ptolemy IX.

- The Romans killed the daughter of Ptolemy XII, because she tried to take over the throne, and she asked Julius Caesar for help.

- Cleopatra VII (yes, the right Cleopatra – the one we'll be talking about in the next chapter) probably had something to do with the death of her husband (and brother). Her goal was to promote her son Ptolemy XV to the throne and, that way, to protect him from the Romans.

The Romans were very much involved in Egypt's internal affairs and had helped many times to different Ptolemies. But the time had come to collect the debts.

Chapter 6 – A Romance, Politics, and Tragedy: The Story of Cleopatra VII

Cleopatra's father, Ptolemy XII, was weak, cruel, and highly unpopular ruler who often relied on the help from Rome to keep him on the throne. His eldest daughter Berenice had already swept him out of the throne once, but he managed to return. He died in 52 BC. His younger daughter, Cleopatra VII, married Ptolemy XIII, who was still a boy, and she thus became the sovereign ruler of Egypt.

Cleopatra and Julius Caesar

At the beginning, the Egyptian people loved Cleopatra. She cared about the people too and was the only ruler in the dynasty that spoke Egyptian. However, once her husband grew up, he managed to turn the populace against her by fraud. His associates distributed a decree in her name that all existing grain should be sent to Alexandria and none to the rest of Egypt. As a result, Cleopatra had to leave and find shelter in Ashkelon in Syria. In 48 BC, she raised an army and came to the border of Egypt, to take her brother/husband Ptolemy XIII down from the throne. The situation was so tense that Julius Caesar had to come to Alexandria to mediate. His goal was to help Cleopatra take the throne. Ptolemy's men tried to frighten Caesar by killing one of his friends and delivering the head as a gift. As a response, Caesar entered the city and took control over the palace. He ordered both Ptolemy and Cleopatra to discharge their armies and meet him. Cleopatra knew Ptolemy wouldn't let her enter Alexandria alive. So she entered hidden inside an oriental rug, which was delivered to Caesar as a gift. Caesar and Cleopatra became lovers, Ptolemy felt betrayed, and after six months of siege, the latter was drowned in the Nile. Cleopatra then married another boy, her brother Ptolemy XIV. Her relationship with Julius Caesar continued, and she gave birth to a son named Ptolemy Caesar, son of Julius Caesar and Cleopatra, also known as Caesarion.

A sculpted relief in the temple of Hathor at Denderah shows Cleopatra presenting her son to the gods to confirm that he was the heir to the throne.

The relationship with Caesar deepened over time; she spent two years in his palace, where she was given a number of gifts and titles. After Julius Caesar was murdered, she escaped back to Egypt, probably arranged the murder of her husband, and married her son, to make sure he would end up on the throne. Meanwhile, the Roman Empire became divided among Octavian, Marcus Lepidus, and Marcus Antonius.

Cleopatra and Marcus Antonius

Cleopatra and Marcus Antonius had already met once, when he visited Egypt with Caesar. The Romans met her father; Cleopatra was only 15 at the time. In 42 BC, they met again. She was 28 and he over 40. They became lovers and, according to Plutarch, they had fantastic time together. After a couple of years, Cleopatra gave birth to twins: Alexander Helios (the sun) and Cleopatra Selene (the moon). Antonius acknowledged paternity of the children. Later he even offered Alexander to marry the daughter of Armenian king, trying to appease a quarrel. The king of Armenia declined, and as a response, Antonius attacked him in 34 BC. Meanwhile, Octavian (later, the Emperor Augustus) had married his sister Octavia to Antonius, to keep him away from Egypt, but his endeavors were futile. In 36 BC in Antioch, Syria, Marcus Antonius and Cleopatra married dressed as the gods Osiris and Isis, the major deities from the myth of creation. Then Cleopatra gave birth to another boy, Ptolemy Philadelphus. In 34 BC, Antonius gave his children amazing titles and power. Alexander Helios became the king of Armenia; Cleopatra Selene became the queen of Cyrenaica and Crete, and Ptolemy Philadelphus became the king of Syria.

Octavian, just like the Romans in general, was upset by Antonius's actions. He decided to take the throne to himself and deal with Antonius and Cleopatra. As a result, in 31 BC, he fought Antonius's and Cleopatra's armies in a sea battle off the coast of Actium (northern Greece). When it became clear that they were losing,

Cleopatra escaped and Antonius followed. The Romans were certain that it is a proof that Marcus Antonius was enslaved by his affection of Cleopatra, incapable of thinking or acting on his own.

In 30 BC, Octavian entered Alexandria. Marcus Antonius welcomed him with his weakened soldiers and navy, which, as soon as they saw the Romans, changed sides. Eventually, Antonius was left alone. Meanwhile, Cleopatra locked herself in her tomb and sent the message to Antony that she was dead. As a response, Antony tried to kill himself. His suicide attempt was now quite successful, but he did end up with a fatal wound, bleeding to death. Then he heard Cleopatra was actually alive, and demanded that to be taken to her instantly. Marcus Antonius died in Cleopatra's arms.

At the same time, Octavian had conquered Alexandria and taken charge of Cleopatra's palace. He planned to take Cleopatra to Rome and drag her through the streets in chains. The Romans couldn't enter the tomb. Cleopatra didn't let Octavian in, but negotiated with him through the closed door, demanding that her kingdom be handed to her children. While Cleopatra's attention was focused on the door, Octavian's men raised ladders and entered through the window. The queen of Egypt immediately attempted to stab herself, but the soldiers quickly disarmed her and imprisoned her and the children. However, Octavian permitted Cleopatra to bury Antonius in royal style. After the funeral Cleopatra stayed in bed, tormented by grief. She firmly decided to die and unite with her love on the other side, so she arranged for a basket of figs concealing an asp to be taken to her. Dying of the asp's venom, the queen wrote a letter to Octavian requesting to be buried in Antonius's tomb. After her death, the only person that could possess any threat to Octavian was Caesarion, but Octavian quickly got rid of him. From that point, Egypt belonged to the Romans.

Cleopatra's death in 30 BC opened the path to Egypt for the Romans to take charge. Nevertheless, Egypt did not become a Roman province, in the true sense of the word, immediately. Octavian used the country as a personal estate. Egypt turned into the main source of grain to the Roman Empire.

But Egypt's significance to Rome was not limited to its agricultural and mineral wealth. The country had access to both the Mediterranean and Red seas, and played a crucial role in Roman commerce—particularly trade with India, the source of the oriental luxuries that the ruling class loved so much. Egypt had a unique strategic position, at the nexus of paths linking Arabia, Asia, Africa, and Europe. This position might have been a crucial reason for Egypt's power and wealth as an independent nation. Ironically, the same geographical advantage ensured Egypt's fall by a succession of other empires. Rome, Byzantium, and Persia – they all saw Egypt as a source of wealth and a trading hub without peer – and so did the Caliphs, the Ottomans, and the British.

The End

The rulers who followed Octavian on the throne of Egypt tried to rule in traditional Egyptian way. They built temples to traditional Egyptian gods, and even represented themselves as Egyptian pharaohs while performing customary rituals. Even though the Egyptian culture changed so much due to the Hellenistic invasion by Alexander, a number of the Egyptian cults were preserved under the Roman rule. Philae temple was still in use in AD 394. This temple held the last inscription written in hieroglyphs in Egypt. 1,400 years passed before anyone could decipher it.

Chapter 7 – The Religion, Mythology, and Rituals of Ancient Egyptians

It may sound confusing that ancient Egyptians had at least 700 different gods (some sources even mention 2000 gods) but not everybody worshiped all the gods, all the time. Each god symbolized and personified a unique concept, function, or place where they were worshiped. People could choose a deity that suited their particular needs.

The religious practice of ancient Egyptians was strictly divided. State religion was all about the king and his divinity. The main, state gods were worshiped in large temples that were closed to the public. The king and the priests are the only people who could enter the temples such as Karnak, Luxor, Abydos, and Abu Simbel, and this sacred practice was effectively inaccessible to others. The ordinary people of Egypt worshiped other gods at their homes, outside the temples, without the priests.

Contrary to popular stereotype, the Egyptians did not actually believe their gods looked like the bizarre creatures represented on old images and hieroglyphs—animals or humans with inanimate objects instead of heads, or humans with animal heads. The goddess Hathor was indeed represented as a woman with the head of a cow, but only to emphasize her motherly nature. Similarly, the goddess Sekhmet's head was lioness's to highlight her aggressiveness. Selket's scorpion body demonstrated that she was the guardian goddess that protects against scorpion and spider bites. The images of other goods, in the same way, serve to inform us of their characteristics as well as their roles in the pantheon. Moreover, one god was often represented in a number of ways. The sun god Ra was either Khepri (beetle-headed human that symbolizes the sun at dawn) or Aten (the sun disc at noon), or Re-Horakhti (a man with falcon's head, or the sun on the horizon) or Flesh (a ram-headed creature and the sun at sunset).

The solar cult, which included worshiping the deities that were related to the solar circle, was especially important in all kingdoms and dynasties. That was because the Egyptians depended on the Sun—the incredibly powerful force that affected their lives. The solar gods are seen as creator gods, and were also closely linked with death the rebirth of the dead. Those gods could also help people increase their fortune and power. Because of this, and to demonstrate their divine origins, the kings included "son of Ra" in their titles.

The explanation for the fact that the Egyptians used to have so many gods lies in the fact they could mix and match their gods with others, by combining their attributes. When a god represented more than one characteristic, he or she was represented in two or more different deities. Amun-Ra, for example, was a mix of Amun, the creator god, and Ra, the solar god. Furthermore, some gods represent combinations of Egyptian and foreign deities: Seth (chaos) with the Canaanite Ball (lightning); Hathor (mother) with the Syrian Anat (marital); Osiris (god of the dead) with the Greek Dionysus (fertility); Isis (mother) with the Greek Aphrodite (love): and Imhotep (medicine) with the Greek Asklepios (also medicine).

The Fight between Order and Chaos: The Central Mythological Narrative

This multitude of deities, cults, and religious stories is unified through a small number of basic mythological themes. Unfortunately, the Egyptians did not have a single holy book, and most of the inscriptions at the temples were all about kings and their offerings to gods. National myths in form of a long narrative were never recovered. All the material that we have about those narratives comes from funerary texts that had the purpose of easing the transition into the afterlife. These sources contain a small number of mythological stories that occur over and over. The details vary from source to source, but basically they all tell the same story.[viii]

- Creator comes into being in the nun (the primordial ocean, a watery chaos personified into a god). The primeval waters were dark and formless, but they held the potential for life just like chaos held the potential for order.[ix] The waters of Nun retreat to reveal the first land (primordial mound), which rises from the nun. (1) The sun god emerges; the solar child is born; first sunrise occurs. Forces of chaos threaten the solar child; then protective deities save the child.[x] (2) The primordial mound is the setting for creation. The creator god Atum (usually depicted wearing the double crown of kingship) emerges at the same time, sitting on the mound. This god is the creator of both Universe and ancient Egypt's political system.[xi]

- Living beings are created from either the bodily fluids, or thoughts, or words, or hands of the creator. The humans originate from Ra's tears. The air god separates the earth god and the sky goddess. Egypt is created as an element of the divine order. The war between chaos (*isfet*) and order (*maat*) continues.

- The creator sun god loses either his eye, or daughter, or defender, but she is persuaded to return. The sun god is mad at disobeying people and gods, and decides to destroy most of humanity and preserve the earth for heaven. Osiris, the mythical ruler of Egypt, is killed by his brother Seth. Osiris's sisters, Isis and Nephthys, are trying to find his damaged body. Isis finds the body and revives Osiris in order to conceive a son, Horus. The body of Osiris is mummified and protected from Seth's assaults. Isis, the divine mother, gives birth to Horus in the marshes. The creatures of chaos poison the baby Horus, but he is healed. Horus and Seth fight against each other for the right to rule. Seth ends up with wounded testicles. Horus loses an eye, or both eyes, but another god (usually Thoth) restores the damaged eye(s). Horus avenges the death of Osiris. Seth is overpowered. Horus, as a result, becomes king of the living. Osiris becomes ruler of the underworld and judge of the dead.

- The sun god goes into the underworld every night. The chaos monster Apophis threatens, but various deities and spirits defend the sun god. The sun god joins Osiris. Together, they raise the dead. The sun god ascends in the morning to regenerate creation.

- The creator is tired, and he returns to the primordial ocean. World reverts to chaos.

It is important to emphasize the link between the Egyptian mythological narratives, religious doctrine, and the politics. The earliest creation myths, as well as all subsequent ones, support the notion of the divine nature of Egyptians rulers. Moreover, the first chronology of Egyptian rulers—the one established by Manetho, who first divided the pharaohs into dynasties—highlighted a single, unbroken succession of kings that links them to the moment of creation and the time of the gods. The creator god had set the pattern for kingship and each subsequent pharaoh was a legitimate inheritor of the throne. The reality, as we already know, was different. At periods of national disunity, a number of rulers based in different parts of Egypt were able to claim the title of the pharaoh and to rule at the same time in concurrent, overlapping dynasties.

At the Top of the Pantheon

The three main gods in ancient Egyptian religion are Osiris, Horus, and Seth. Osiris rules the underworld. According to ancient belief, when a king died, he became Osiris and continued to rule in the afterlife. Ancient art represents him as a mummy with the crook and flail, which demonstrate his permanent role as a king. Horus, the god of order, is Osiris's and Isis's son. The king of Egypt held the attributes of this deity. In fact, the Egyptians believed that the pharaoh was an incarnation of Horus on Earth. This god is usually depicted as a man with a hawk head. Seth was the god of chaos and the brother of Osiris, characterized as an awkward-looking human with a curved nose and long ears.

Correspondingly, there are three main goddesses: Isis, Nephthys, and Hathor. Isis, the divine mother, is both the sister and wife to Osiris and the mother of Horus. This goddess is depicted as a beautiful woman with a throne sign on her head, or as a kite, as her role is to provide the breath of life to the deceased. Nephthys. A goddess closely linked with rebirth, is the sister of Isis and Osiris. She helped her sister bring their brother back to life. Nephthys is represented similarly to Isis. Hathor is another mother goddess, the daughter of the sun god Ra, and goddess of love, beauty, fertility, sex, and death (she provides food for the deceased). Hathor is represented in several ways, all including the combination of body parts of a woman and a cow.

Maat was a separate deity that existed in all aspects of ancient Egyptians' lives. She symbolized cosmic balance, justice, and truth. This goddess was illustrated as a human with a feather on her head or just as a feather, because a feather was the hieroglyphic sign for truth. Judges in ancient Egypt were the priests of Maat.

Domestic Gods

It may sound strange, but the broad population did not particularly worship the mythical Horus—for them, their pharaoh was Horus himself—and the deities from the myth of creation. They had their own gods that were much closer to them, and they worshiped them in the home. The way they worshiped them was similar to the rituals in the temples. They kept the statues representing gods in their domestic shrines, and they fed, washed, and anointed them daily.

Hathor was a goddess particularly important in every home, as she was in charge of marriage, sexual love, fertility, conception, and childbirth. There was more than one deity related to fertility and childbirth. Bes, depicted as a dwarf with bowed legs, was regularly invoked during childbirth to ensure a safe birth and protect the mother and the infant. Taweret, the goddess represented as a pregnant hippo, also had a role of protecting women during childbirth.

The craftsmen who built the Valley of the Kings worshiped the creator god Ptah as the patron deity. They relied on this god to help them avoid and cure some work-related issues, such as blindness, which was very common among them, they also worshiped Meretseger, depicted as a cobra or a woman with the head of a cobra, ready to strike. Meretseger was in charge of protecting the people from bites from cobras, spiders, and scorpions.

Daily Rituals

The rituals were identical at all temples and homes in Egypt, regardless of the nature and function of different deities. The people at home did the same as the priests in temples. They entered the sanctuaries twice a day and carried out the rituals. At the moment of sunrise, the priest took the statue from the shrine and washed it, then rubbed it with ointments and perfumes. Finally, the priest dressed the statue in a clean linen shawl, and offered it food and drink. Food and drink were placed at the deity's feet to take spiritual nourishment. After that, the statue was either distributed among the priests in the temple, or among family members at home. In the evening, the same rituals took place. After the statue had been fed, it was put to bed inside the shrine.

The Main Cult Centers

The major deities had their own cult centers that had specific practices, symbols, and prayers. Ra was worshiped at Heliopolis. It looks like his temple was larger than the one at Karnak, but unfortunately, the excavation site is not open to the public at the present moment. Seth cult centers at Avaris and Qantir are also closed to the public. Amun was worshiped nationwide, but his main cult center was the magnificent temple complex at Karnak. Fortunately, we can visit this site, as well as the others such as Osiris's temple at Abydos, Isis's temple at Philae, and Hathor's temple at Denderah. Horus's three main temples were at Edfu, Kom Ombo, and Heliopolis; the first two are open to the public.

Sacred Festivals

A number of festivals took place month after month. They were a crucial part of worship. The largest and most important festivals were: Beautiful Festival of the Valley in Thebes, when families had an opportunity to feast with their dead relatives; Festival of Sokar-Osiris, celebrated as a mortuary or lunar festival at night, when people took offerings to both the god and the dead; Opet Festival at Thebes, which involved a procession from Karnak temple to Luxor temple, along the sphinx avenue, and carrying the statue of Amun; Festival of Drunkenness, different from the above, was celebrated at Deir el Medina and involved five days of drinking in honor of Hathor.

Amulets

Amulets were believed to have the power to protect their wearers and increase their strength. Amulets were figures made of different materials and usually attached to a necklace, bracelet, or ring. There were many different types of amulets, each providing protection of an individual deity from a particular threat. Not all amulets featured images of deities; many of them held symbolic, hieroglyphic signs and were related to specific aspects of mythology. The ankh represented eternal life. Scarabs were associated with the sun, new life, and rebirth. Eye of Horus was believed to protect from all evil forces, spiritual and physical alike. Hedgehogs were believed to help with fertility and rebirth. A leg represented health, because a leg is an element of the hieroglyphic sign for health. Two fingers protected the mummified bodies. Flies helped against insects. Frogs ensured fertility of women. A carpenter's set-square and plumb-line granted eternal virtue and stability.

Amulets also served as status symbols. Wealthy individuals wore amulets made of expensive materials, like faience, or semi-precious stones such as amethyst, onyx, and carnelian.

Execration and Curse Figures

The power of figures was not limited to protection. They also served as a means of destruction. The Pharaoh used execration figures to devastate the political enemies of the country. The figures represented bound captives, each wearing a list of Egypt's traditional enemies (Asiatics, Nubians, Syrians, Libyans) on its torso. The king ritually broke and buried the figures, to ensure the fall of the enemy. Private individuals made curse figures to hurt and immobilize another individual.

Communication with the Deities

The people had a possibility of consulting oracles that provided answers to arguments and numerous personal and legal issues. The Egyptians could talk to oracles in temples or even on the streets, as long as there was a procession with the statue of the god around. People either placed a written message in front of the divine statue at the temple or asked the statue in the procession, which answered through the priests who carried it. The answers were always with ambiguous meanings and were not definitive. People could approach as many oracles as they wanted with the same question.

People also dreamed individual gods, but needed the help of the priests to interpret the meaning of the dreams. The priests answered their concerns, told them what they were supposed to do, and people, in turn, gave contributions to the temple.

The Cult of Ancestors and Deified Humans

In Egyptian villages, people honored the deceased family members and appealed to them for help with everyday issues. They believed that their ancestors had both the power to influence the lives of the living and to convey their messages to the gods of the afterlife. Because of that, the Egyptians kept their dead in close proximity, and included them in everyday activities and family meals. Most sitting rooms had false doors incorporated, to enable the ancestor's spirit to enter the home. Furthermore, the figures called ancestral busts, which represented the deceased ancestors, were placed in household shrines and taken to religious festivals and processions.

Some notable individuals were worshiped widely and addressed for reasons such as fertility, childbirth, and moral leadership. Famous deified humans were Imhotep, who was actually an architect (he built the step pyramid at Saqqara) but was deified as a god of medicine; Senworsret III, who founded the city of Kahun for the workers who worked on his pyramid; Amenhotep was worshiped in Deir el Medina because he founded the village; another Amenhotep, the vizier during the reign of pharaoh Amenhotep III was revered and worshipped for his wisdom; Horemheb was deified by Ramses II, who was thankful because Horemheb gave the throne to his grandfather, even though they weren't family.

Chapter 8 – Funerary Beliefs and Rituals: Mummification and Afterlife

Ancient Egyptians, just like people of all times and places, loved life. They wanted to live forever and believed they could achieve eternal life. According to their beliefs, an individual could make his or her life after death even better and more prosperous than the life before, as long they were well prepared for it. For them, the afterlife was the so-called *Field of Reeds*, which looked exactly like the earthly Egypt. The solar cycle was essential for the afterlife, because the dead would lay in primordial darkness if it weren't for the sun god who visited them each night.

The Elements of a Human Being

An individual, according to ancient Egyptians, was created from six components, which were separated at the moment of death. To ensure a successful resurrection, these elements needed to be reunited. This was achieved through the funerary customs. The six parts of a human were: the ka (life force), the ba (personality), the akh (spirit—the successful union of the ka and ba), the name (identity), the shadow (related to the solar cult; no sun – no shadow), and the body (contains all elements and needs to be preserved by the process of mummification).

The Pharaoh's Curse

Hollywood movies are to be blamed for negative imagery around mummies, but not just Hollywood. When in 1922 Howard Carter and his team started the excavation of the tomb of Tutankhamun, they made use of the superstition of local people and the popular myth that entering that tomb would activate an ancient curse. They knew that, if the locals believed the curse was true, they wouldn't enter the tomb at night. So one day an English newspaper spread the word about the curse and, from that day, every time a person who happened to be a member of the excavation team died, even after 20 years, the public blamed the curse. The only death that was a bit awkward was the one of Lord Carnarvon, who passed out because of an infected insect bite. The excavation was not completely over at that point, and he was the one who sponsored it. At the time of his death, an electrical blackout happened in Cairo (which actually happens quite often), and many have interpreted this as a sure sign of the curse.

Nevertheless, even though there is no curse related to the tomb of Tutankhamun; thousands of tombs have been excavated in Egypt, and only two of them (of Harkkhuf of the sixth dynasty and Ursa from early New Kingdom) contain curses in their inscriptions, to protect them from robbers. Egyptologists and historians seem to be safe, as they spread the word about the glory of pharaohs. According to ancient Egyptian religious doctrine, the repetition of a name ensures a prolonged afterlife.

Mummification in Practice

In the pre-dynastic period, the Egyptian customs involved burying the dead in shallow pits in the sand on the desert edge. These burial places weren't particularly arranged. The bodies were unwrapped and placed directly into the sand in a fetal position. The only funerary goods at that time were pots containing food and drink. Sometimes animals exposed the bodies, which were naturally preserved by the sand, and the Egyptians came up with the idea to ensure the preservation of the dead. During the next thousand years the Egyptians experimented with various mummification methods. Bodies were buried inside large clay pots, on shallow reed trays, or wrapped in animal skins. These methods didn't work. Since the bodies were isolated from the sand, which naturally preserved them, the soft tissues disintegrated. The Egyptians learned they needed to preserve the bodies before the burial. The first properly mummified body was the one of the pharaoh Djer of the first dynasty. Needless to say, mummification was available as an option only to the elite, while the others were still just being buried in the sand.

Herodotus gives us a detailed account of the mummification process and the role of a new kind of professional: the embalmer. Embalmers had their workshops in local cemetery sites. The senior embalmers were highly respected priests. The most senior embalmer wore a jackal mask, which represented the god of embalming, Anubis. However, according to Herodotus, the bodies of rich and powerful women, especially queens, were usually kept at their palaces for a couple of days before being taken to the workshop, to prevent the bodies from being defiled.

The pharaohs and, since the Middle Kingdom, the nobles, wanted to look like Osiris when they die. This request involved the most complicated and expensive process that involved removing the brain (the Egyptians believed that preserving the brain was unnecessary, because the thoughts and emotions occurred in the heart). This operation was performed in several very creative ways. The contents of the abdomen were removed too, with the exception of the heart. This job was not only gross but also dangerous, because the embalmer who did that part of the work was chased out of the workshop as a part of the ceremony, during which people threw stones and sticks at him. The royal abdomen was then cleaned with wine and spices, filled with aromatic substances and linen, and finally sewn up. The viscera were also preserved and kept in canopic jars. The bodies were wrapped 35-40 days after the preservation.

Large amounts of linen were used; some mummies were covered with more than 40 layers of the most expensive linen. The styles of wrapping varied and evolved over time, from wrapping each limb separately in the Old Kingdom; all limbs wrapped together and covered with a mummy mask in the Middle Kingdom; all the way to the portraits that were put among the wrappings in the Roman era.

It was of course not enough to preserve the bodies. Additional safety measures were included in the tombs to guarantee that nothing obstructed the deceased on their journey to rebirth and the afterlife. Guidebooks contained instructions that gave all necessary information to the deceased, and were inscribed on papyri, coffins, bandages, and walls. The earliest funerary texts are the pyramid texts. They were written in the burial chamber and antechamber of the pyramid and did not include any pictures. The green color of hieroglyphs represented regeneration. In the Middle Kingdom, the coffin texts were introduced, and the New Kingdom brought *The Book of the Dead* and the *Guides to the Hereafter*, each containing detailed instructions as well as numerous spells to help the deceased change the side swiftly, as well as to make his or her new life as good as possible.

Chapter 9 – The Architecture of Ancient Egypt: Temples and Pyramids

Temples

The temples were the most eye-catching structures on the ancient Egyptian landscape. Nevertheless, the public had no access to them; only the priests and the royal family could enter these magnificent places. There were two types of temples. Cult temples or houses of god were usually located on the east bank of the Nile and most of them were dedicated to one specific deity. Mortuary temples, on the other hand, were built to enable king's worshipers to keep his spirit nourished for the afterlife. They were also called temples of millions of years and were situated on the west bank of the Nile.

The Egyptians believed that the design of temples – just everything else – was defined in the remote past by the gods. Therefore they never changed the design of the temples, but instead they constructed bigger and bigger versions of the same designs.

The first temple in Egypt was built around 3200 BC at Hierakonpolis near Luxor. The deity worshiped at this temple was probably Horus, although no proofs were found of that. The temple was built on a raised mound of sand, which most probably was a symbolical representation of primordial mound. At Medamud near Thebes was another ancient cult temple, but it remains unclear which god was worshiped there.

The Middle Kingdom temples were very simple and symmetrical, but unfortunately most of them were destroyed in antiquity and replaced with new ones in the New Kingdom. The Karnak temple is special, because its design dates from the Middle Kingdom, but it also features New Kingdom influences. This temple – the largest religious center in the world – was built over the period of 2000 years. It is important to highlight that the ideal, traditional Egyptian temple is designed in the Middle Kingdom. The New Kingdom brought new conventions and the temples built during this period were more stylized than the ones before.

A panorama of the great hypostyle hall at Karnak

Many temples are improved by adding processional avenues or sphinx avenues, because they were lined by the statues of various sphinxes, such as ram-headed lions that represented the god Amun; falcon-headed lions, which represented Horus; human-headed lions that represented the pharaoh who constructed them; sphinxes with the head of a crocodile (representing the god Sobek), jackal (Anubis), or snake (the cobra goddess Wadjet). The last few sphinxes were found only at one temple – the mortuary temple of Amenhotep III at Luxor. The best-known processional avenue is the one between the temples at Luxor and Karnak. Many other temples, such as Abu Simbel in Nubia, also had such avenues, but unfortunately, they haven't been preserved.

During religious festivals, the priests walked through the avenues, carrying the sacred bark on their shoulders, but the public couldn't see them. Behind the two rows of sphinxes, there was also a wall. It was complicated to enter the temple. The entrance was always at the lowest point of the temple, and the priests needed to follow a fairly complex system of staircases or ramps in order to get to the sanctuary, which was always located at the rear.

Philae Temple[xii]

Because the temples were inaccessible to the public, it wasn't easy to get into them. The exterior of the temple was uninviting by design and all temples were enclosed by huge walls, made of mud-bricks, which were sometimes more than 10 meters wide. These barriers kept people out efficiently, but they also offered protection during times of war or conflict for the royal family and priests.

The most important part of a temple was the sanctuary, the inner sanctum, or the Holy of Holies, which was placed at the highest point of the temple. The only people who were allowed to enter the sanctuary were the king and the high priest. Inside the sanctuary, an altar with a small shrine with golden or bronze doors protected the cult statue. For the Egyptians, this statue was not just a depiction of the god; it was home to the spirit of the god. That is why access to the statue was strictly prohibited for the populace.

Each temple represented the universe. Each sanctuary symbolized the primordial mound. Furthermore, a secret lake inside every temple represented the primordial waters. The water was used for the purification of the priests and the temple as well as in ritual offerings.

It is not easy for today's visitors to imagine what the temples originally looked like. The existing ruins appear like open, bright places. However, this impression is far from how the temples looked in ancient times. All the temple areas – excluding the sacred lake and first pillared hall – were covered with heavy stone roofs. The doors were large, heavy, and extremely difficult to penetrate. There weren't any windows. The light came in either through small holes inside the ceiling blocks, or from stone grilles up on the walls. In special occasions, the priests used oil lamps. The interior of a temple was without any doubt a dark and gloomy place.

A temple complex contained many outbuildings, which were important for the function of the temple. These outbuildings included the stores, kitchens, houses for the priests, stables, and, from the Ptolemaic period, the mammissi (birth house) and sanatorium.

The statue in the shrine was not the only sacred object that showed the devotion to the gods. Pharaohs also utilized painted or carved decoration, numerous statues, and obelisks. Obelisks were tall, needle-like structures made from a single block of stone, and each temple had at least two of them.

All ritual activities inside the temple were related to the secret statue in the sanctuary. The pharaoh was formally the high priest of all the cults in every temple in Egypt. His duty was to perform all the essential rituals required to maintain the cosmic order, or Maat. If the king neglected his duty to the gods, the country would fall into a state of chaos, including floods, famine, or invasion. The pharaoh, however, delegated this duty. Each temple had a separate high priest, but these priests did everything on king's behalf rather than on their own.

Tombs

Egypt is famous for its burial sites, pyramids and tombs, both referred to as Houses of Eternity, in the Valley of the Kings. The Valley tombs are developed as the result of ages of evolution brought on by shifting religious priorities and growing security risks. All of them were meant to last for eternity, as a home for the deceased in the afterlife. None of them is actually complete. No tomb in the Valley of Kings or in entire Egypt is finished. Some of them were carved entirely out of the rock and never decorated. Others had been drawn, but the carving never started. Many tombs gave the impression of complete work, but the inscriptions or images are missing. The work in most cases was probably interrupted by the death of the intended recipient. Moreover, to complete a tomb would be to claim perfection, and looks like ancient Egyptian architects weren't keen to make such claim.

Based on the style, Egyptologists are sometimes able to tell the period when a tomb was built. However, literally all the tombs were robbed in ancient times. Sometimes the priest had to move the bodies to other buildings, to prevent further violation. A number of tombs do not contain bodies or grave goods.

Pyramids

Pyramids have become the synonym of ancient Egypt long ago. These structures were portrayed in many books and popular movies, but most often not in the way they deserve.

The function of pyramids was always funerary, but the details changed over time. In the Old and Middle Kingdom, pyramids served as tombs, which also showed the wealth and status of the deceased. In the New Kingdom, the pyramids were smaller and were used to surmount a tomb. They were not functioning as burial places.

The shape of the pyramid is significant itself. It is, in fact, a stylization of the primordial mound, called a benben, which was closely associated with the sun god. The pyramidal shape was thought to resemble the rays of the sun. Furthermore, the Pyramid Texts refer to the pyramid as a ramp leading to the sky, allowing the deceased pharaoh to join his ancestors.

The first pyramid was built at Meidum, near present-day Cairo, by the first pharaoh of the fourth dynasty, called Sneferu. The burial chamber of this pyramid had never been completed, and Snefery was most likely buried in one of the remaining two pyramids he built. Those pyramids are located at Dashur and are known as the Bent Pyramid (due to a change in design that went wrong) and the Red or North Pyramid. The latter was the first successfully constructed pyramid. It still exists at the site of Dashur, and it is huge; only the Great Pyramid of Khufu at Giza is bigger than it.

Khufu, the son of Sneferu, outperformed his father's project with his pyramid at the new site of Giza, called the Great Pyramid. It was listed as one of the seven wonders of the ancient world. The bodies of the three queens of Khufu were buried in three satellite pyramids set in close proximity, on the east of the major pyramid. The pyramid complex still attracts a number of tourists from around the world. Khafra, the son of Khufu, knew he couldn't compete with the monumentality of his father's pyramid, and he did something else instead. He placed his construction on a higher area, which gave it the appearance of being bigger even though it is not. The next pharaoh buried at the Giza plateau was Menkaura. His pyramid is not as large of the previous two, but it was made of granite and limestone and therefore very valuable. On the other hand, Menkaura's temples were larger than those of his ancestors. Another monumental object at the Giza plateau is the giant sphinx with a lion's body and a human head, which obviously had the function of guardian.

The fifth-dynasty pharaohs, Unas and Djoser, built their pyramids at Saqqara. While the pyramid complex of Unas represents a perfect example of the fully developed form, the Djoser's pyramid is better preserved.

In the Middle Kingdom, many kings had complexes at sites such as Dashur, Lisht, El Lahur, and Hawara. In the New Kingdom, however, pharaohs were no longer buried in pyramids. They used secretive rock-cut tombs. The last development in pyramid evolution occurred at Abydos and Thebes during the reign of the 26th dynasty pharaohs. Notable new pyramids were no longer built, but many of the old ones still endure to remind humanity of its impermanence.

Conclusion – Exciting Excavations and Global Egyptomania: Why Are We So Obsessed with Ancient Egypt?

Egypt has had a distinctive charm since the times of ancient Greeks and Romans, who referred to it as a far older civilization, full of wonderful and mysterious monuments and inscriptions. They seemed to believe that Egyptian culture had arisen entirely formed and had disappeared just as abruptly.[xiii] However, its 3,000-year history throws a long shadow over subsequent centuries and we can still sense it today. The fascination with ancient Egypt continued in the Renaissance and flourished in the time of Napoleon, when the famous Rosetta Stone was discovered. In 1822, Champollion identified and deciphered the inscriptions on the stone and thus unlocked the secrets to the history of Ancient Egypt. In the 19th century, almost every notable person descended on the Nile, including Gustave Flaubert and Ulysses S. Grant. The interest had been heat up by the translation of the Rosetta Stone, which finally revealed most of what we know of the history of Ancient Egypt. Most, but not all. The real obsession had started a year later, in 1922, when magnificent artifacts were exhumed from Tutankhamun's tomb.

In late November of 1922, the English Egyptologist Howard Carter, accompanied by his patron, George Herbert, fifth Earl of Carnarvon, his daughter, Lady Evelyn, and Carter's friend, the engineer Arthur Callender, discovered an intact tomb from the age known as the New

Kingdom, a time of mighty pharaohs and beautiful queens. That was the last hidden tomb in the Valley of the Kings, and the most attractive one. Its seals remained intact from the antique times, and it contained treasures of inconceivable luxury. The hieroglyphs on many of the objects clearly spelled out the name of the tomb owner: Tut-ankh-Amun. The king's burial rested within, having been undisturbed for the lengthy period of thirty-three centuries.

Replica of the golden mask of Tutankhamun in the Egyptian Museum[xiv]

The greatest discovery in the history of Egyptology had been made, and it was the first major archaeological discovery to be covered by the world's press. Newspaper headlines captured the public imagination and generated a wave of popular interest in the pharaohs' treasures. But it was only the beginning. It took a year before lifting the one-and-a-quarter-ton lid from the pharaoh's colossal stone sarcophagus was possible. Inside the sarcophagus, three nested coffins complemented the four gilded shrines in protecting the king's body. All coffins were filled with precious amulets and ritual objects, and the innermost coffin was made of pure gold. The boy king's mummified remains as well as his astonishing funerary mask—probably the most splendid artifact ever recovered from an ancient civilization[xv]—were revealed three years after the initial discovery. Meanwhile, the Earl of Carnarvon had died from blood poisoning and the nutshell of the stories that involved the curse of the pharaoh had been generated.

The global fascination with the ancient Egyptian civilization endured and is still present today. According to the author of "Egyptomania", the obsession is based "on the fact that it is both comfortably familiar and intriguingly exotic."[xvi]

Check out another book by Captivating History

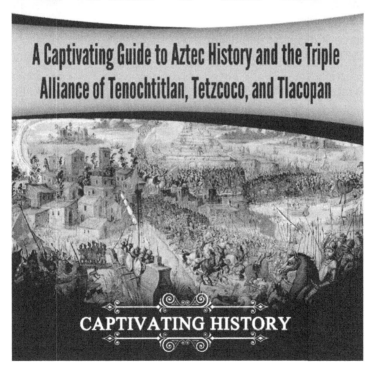

References

[i] This general chronology is widely accepted; source: Clayton, Peter, *Chronicle of the Pharaohs*, Thames and Hudson Press

[ii] Wilkinson

[iii] The Satire of the Trades, or The Instruction of Dua-Kheti, is an Instruction by a scribe named Dua-Kheti for his son Pepi. Transliteration from Egyptian script as well as translation into English is available online: http://www.ucl.ac.uk/museums-static/digitalegypt//literature/satiretransl.html Retrieved January 13, 2018

[iv] Different sources offer different years. It is now certain that Narmer united Egypt at some point between 3100 and 2950 BC

[v] The source text is available online at http://www.reshafim.org.il/ad/egypt/texts/ipuwer.htm Retrieved January 17, 2018

[vi] A colossal statue of Akhenaten from his Aten Temple at Karnak. Egyptian Museum of Cairo. Image courtesy of Gérard Ducher, source: Wikimedia Commons

[vii] Image courtesy by Istanbul Museum of Archaeology

[viii] The primordial mythical narrative according to Geraldine Pinch, *Egyptian Myth, A Very Short Introduction*, Oxford University Press, 2004

[ix] Wilkinson (*Rise and Fall of Ancient Egypt*) associates the myth of Nun with the Nile—the water that has literally always been the source of life.

[x] Pinch

[xi] Wilkinson

[xii] Image courtesy of Marc Ryckaert, source: Wikimedia Commons

[xiii] Fritze, Ronald H., *Egyptomania: A History of Fascination, Obsession and Fantasy*, Reaktion Books/University of Chicago Press, 2016

[xiv] Image courtesy by Carsten Frenzl, Flickr – via Wikimedia Commons https://commons.wikimedia.org/wiki/File:TUT-Ausstellung_FFM_2012_47_(7117819557).jpg

[xv] Wilkinson, Toby, *The Rise and Fall of Ancient Egypt*, Random House, 2011

[xvi] Fritze

Free Bonus from Captivating History (Available for a Limited time)

Hi History Lovers!

Now you have a chance to join our exclusive history list so you can get your first history ebook for free as well as discounts and a potential to get more history books for free! Simply visit the link below to join.

Captivatinghistory.com/ebook

Also, make sure to follow us on:

Twitter: @Captivhistory

Facebook: Captivating History: @captivatinghistory

ABOUT CAPTIVATING HISTORY

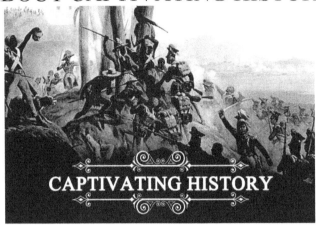

A lot of history books just contain dry facts that will eventually bore the reader. That's why Captivating History was created. Now you can enjoy history books that will mesmerize you. But be careful though, hours can fly by, and before you know it; you're up reading way past bedtime.

Get your first history book for free here:
http://www.captivatinghistory.com/ebook

Make sure to follow us on Twitter: @CaptivHistory
and Facebook: www.facebook.com/captivatinghistory so you can get all of our updates!

.

Made in the USA
Monee, IL
25 November 2022